A PERSONAL GROWTH JOURNAL FOR WOMEN

ALICIA JENNINGS

www.empowerherstory.com

This journal is dedicated to the woman who wants to get rid of self-limiting beliefs.
To the woman who wants to cultivate a positive mindset.
To the woman who wants to embrace her individuality.
To the woman who wants to prioritize self-care.
To the woman who wants to get to know herself better.
To the woman who wants to turn her dreams into reality.

This journal is dedicated to all the women who are committed to becoming the best version of themselves.

EMPOWER HER STORY

Dear Storyteller,

Welcome to *Nurture Your Soul: A Personal Growth Journal for Women.* I am so happy that you are here! This journal was created to guide you towards a more happy, healthy, and purposeful life.

Nurture Your Soul includes a mix of **gentle reminders** to support you on your journey, **journaling prompts** to encourage introspection, **blank pages** to encourage creativity, and **self care practices** to help you improve your mental, physical, and emotional well being.

Journaling became a powerful tool for me during my teen years. I didn't feel comfortable sharing my truths with my family or friends but every time I wrote, I felt free. I felt empowered. Over the years, journaling has helped me explore my inner voice and it has taught me to be more authentic. I've grown to love guided journaling the most because it constantly helps me get to know myself better.

As you fill up these pages with love, pain, passion, joy, perseverance, and purpose, remember to enjoy the journey. Don't feel pressured to show up perfectly. This is your safe space to flow freely. *Nurture Your Soul* is designed for you to journal and practice self care at least once a week but feel free to create your own routine. There is no right or wrong way to use this journal.

My only hope is that you'll finish this journal with a better sense of self. Now go grab your cutest pen, a lavender candle, and come write with me!

With love,

Alicia

I, ______________________________,

NAME

promise to create the life I desire.

I vow to love, heal, and discover myself by any means necessary.

EMPOWER HER STORY

Connect with Alicia Jennings

Instagram: @empower_herstory
Twitter: @aliciaannj
Facebook: Empower Her Story
Website: empowerherstory.com

To share your writing on social media, use the hashtag #writewithalicia

EMPOWER HER STORY

Nothing can *grow* without proper maintenance. Take care of **yourself**.

EMPOWER HER STORY

JOURNAL PROMPT

Why is starting over beautiful?

EMPOWER HER STORY

DATE

DATE

GENTLE REMINDER

You are allowed to reinvent yourself as many times as you'd like.

ALICIA JENNINGS

SELF CARE IDEA

Start learning a new skill. Indulge in a topic you enjoy just for fun!

EXPRESS YOURSELF

EMPOWER HER STORY

JOURNAL PROMPT

What is the nicest thing you've done for yourself? What are you planning to do next?

DATE

DATE

GENTLE REMINDER

It's okay to choose yourself. You deserve the love and kindness you give to everyone else.

ALICIA JENNINGS

SELF CARE IDEA

Set the mood while cooking your favorite meal. Light some candles and play your favorite tunes.

EXPRESS YOURSELF

EMPOWER HER STORY

JOURNAL PROMPT

What are you afraid of? Make a list of everything that scares you.

DATE

DATE

Don't let fear of what could happen make nothing happen.

ALICIA JENNINGS

SELF CARE IDEA

Plan an adventure and visit a new place.

EXPRESS YOURSELF

EMPOWER HER STORY

JOURNAL PROMPT

How do you envision your future? Where do you see yourself in one year?

DATE

DATE

GENTLE REMINDER

Your dreams are not real until you write them down.

ALICIA JENNINGS

SELF CARE IDEA

Create a vision board. List every goal you want to achieve this year.

EMPOWER HER STORY

EXPRESS YOURSELF

EMPOWER HER STORY

JOURNAL PROMPT

Who taught you about love and what did they teach you?

DATE

DATE

GENTLE REMINDER

Love yourself fully as you continue to grow.

ALICIA JENNINGS

SELF CARE IDEA

Determine your love language by taking the 5 love languages quiz.

EXPRESS YOURSELF

EMPOWER HER STORY

JOURNAL PROMPT

How are you feeling right now? Be honest with yourself.

DATE

DATE

GENTLE REMINDER

Allow your feelings to flow with ease.

ALICIA JENNINGS

SELF CARE IDEA

Find a guided meditation online and meditate for 10 minutes.

EXPRESS YOURSELF

EMPOWER HER STORY

JOURNAL PROMPT

What is one thing you would do if you knew you could not fail?

DATE

DATE

GENTLE REMINDER

You don't need to have everything figured out.

ALICIA JENNINGS

SELF CARE IDEA

Choose your favorite self care activity today.

EMPOWER HER STORY

EXPRESS YOURSELF

EMPOWER HER STORY

JOURNAL PROMPT

Ask someone close to you what they love about you. Write it down here.

DATE

DATE

GENTLE REMINDER

You are not for everybody. Everybody is not for you.

ALICIA JENNINGS

SELF CARE IDEA

Spend 30 minutes in solitude. No electronic devices allowed!

EXPRESS YOURSELF

EMPOWER HER STORY

JOURNAL PROMPT

What negative beliefs do you hold about yourself that you need to let go of?

DATE

DATE

GENTLE REMINDER

You are more than enough. You don't have to conform to make other people feel comfortable.

ALICIA JENNINGS

SELF CARE IDEA

Move your body! Exercise for 30 minutes at home or go to the gym.

EXPRESS YOURSELF

EMPOWER HER STORY

JOURNAL PROMPT

What risks do you want to take this year? What's holding you back?

DATE

DATE

GENTLE REMINDER

You can't grow in your comfort zone.

ALICIA JENNINGS

Try a new activity this week! (Dance class, cooking class, yoga class etc.)

EXPRESS YOURSELF

EMPOWER HER STORY

JOURNAL PROMPT

How can you start putting yourself first each day?

DATE

DATE

Pour into yourself today, tomorrow, forever. You deserve a full cup.

ALICIA JENNINGS

SELF CARE IDEA

Do one thing that contributes to your personal growth today.

EXPRESS YOURSELF

EMPOWER HER STORY

JOURNAL PROMPT

List the things you need help with. Name one person who can support you.

DATE

DATE

GENTLE REMINDER

You don't have to suffer in silence.

ALICIA JENNINGS

SELF CARE IDEA

Take the day off from your everyday responsibilities. Ask a friend to assist you.

EXPRESS YOURSELF

EMPOWER HER STORY

JOURNAL PROMPT

Recall the moment you started to notice that you were becoming your true self.

DATE

DATE

GENTLE REMINDER

You are exactly where you're supposed to be.

ALICIA JENNINGS

SELF CARE IDEA

Write down 3 small wins that made you smile today. Treat yourself to something nice.

EXPRESS YOURSELF

EMPOWER HER STORY

JOURNAL PROMPT

What makes you happy?

EMPOWER HER STORY

DATE

DATE

GENTLE REMINDER

Happiness is a choice. Do what makes you happy everyday.

ALICIA JENNINGS

SELF CARE IDEA

Make a list of fun activities you want to do and post them on your refrigerator.

EXPRESS YOURSELF

EMPOWER HER STORY

JOURNAL PROMPT

What mistakes do you need to forgive yourself for?

DATE

DATE

GENTLE REMINDER

Forgive yourself for not knowing everything you know today.

ALICIA JENNINGS

SELF CARE IDEA

Light a candle, relax and watch your favorite TV show.

EXPRESS YOURSELF

EMPOWER HER STORY

JOURNAL PROMPT

What is a new project/habit you want to start?

DATE

DATE

GENTLE REMINDER

New beginnings are necessary. Resetting, refocusing, and realigning is apart of life.

ALICIA JENNINGS

SELF CARE IDEA

Get some fresh air. Take a 30 minute walk.

EXPRESS YOURSELF

EMPOWER HER STORY

JOURNAL PROMPT

What do you love about yourself? Write yourself a love letter. "Dear self, I love you..."

DATE

DATE

GENTLE REMINDER

Embrace your individuality. You are one of a kind.

ALICIA JENNINGS

SELF CARE IDEA

Buy yourself fresh flowers.

EXPRESS YOURSELF

EMPOWER HER STORY

JOURNAL PROMPT

What do you need to unlearn about perfectionism?

DATE

DATE

Perfect doesn't exist. You are doing way better than you think.

ALICIA JENNINGS

SELF CARE IDEA

Creatively express your feelings. (Write/draw/paint/sing/dance)

EXPRESS YOURSELF

EMPOWER HER STORY

JOURNAL PROMPT

What goals are you working toward? How will you achieve them?

DATE

DATE

GENTLE REMINDER

Your best is
yet to come.
Keep going!

ALICIA JENNINGS

SELF CARE IDEA

Today is a rest day. Make it a priority to relax.

EXPRESS YOURSELF

EMPOWER HER STORY

JOURNAL PROMPT

What makes you smile?

EMPOWER HER STORY

DATE

DATE

GENTLE REMINDER

Speak up for yourself. You matter. Your words, your voice, your life, matters.

ALICIA JENNINGS

SELF CARE IDEA

Create an emotional toolbox. Include anything that makes you smile.

EXPRESS YOURSELF

EMPOWER HER STORY

JOURNAL PROMPT

What secrets are you holding onto and what harm are they causing?

DATE

DATE

GENTLE REMINDER

Healing takes time.

ALICIA JENNINGS

SELF CARE IDEA

Take some time for rest and relaxation.

EMPOWER HER STORY

EXPRESS YOURSELF

EMPOWER HER STORY

JOURNAL PROMPT

What are you still learning?

DATE

DATE

GENTLE REMINDER

No one has it altogether. We are all students. We are all a work in progress.

ALICIA JENNINGS

SELF CARE IDEA

Dedicate 30 minutes to reading a new book.

EXPRESS YOURSELF

EMPOWER HER STORY

JOURNAL PROMPT

Write down 5 affirmations to help you practice self-compassion.

DATE

DATE

GENTLE REMINDER

Give yourself grace. Not all days are going to be picture perfect.

ALICIA JENNINGS

SELF CARE IDEA

Start your day with gratitude. Write down 3 things you are grateful for.

EXPRESS YOURSELF

EMPOWER HER STORY

JOURNAL PROMPT

What are some things you'd like to start saying "NO" to?

DATE

DATE

GENTLE REMINDER

Set boundaries and stick to them. You are responsible for teaching people how to treat you.

ALICIA JENNINGS

SELF CARE IDEA

Create a morning routine. List 3 things you want to do each morning. Get started immediately!

EXPRESS YOURSELF

EMPOWER HER STORY

JOURNAL PROMPT

Write down 5 things you have accomplished that you are proud of.

DATE

DATE

GENTLE REMINDER

Don't rely on others for validation.

ALICIA JENNINGS

SELF CARE IDEA

Celebrate yourself! Buy something you've always wanted.

EXPRESS YOURSELF

EMPOWER HER STORY

JOURNAL PROMPT

Count your blessings. Make a list of everything you have.

DATE

DATE

GENTLE REMINDER

You have everything you need.

ALICIA JENNINGS

SELF CARE IDEA

Think of someone who has made a difference in your life. Write them a thank you note.

EMPOWER HER STORY

EXPRESS YOURSELF

EMPOWER HER STORY

JOURNAL PROMPT

How do you want to be remembered?

DATE

DATE

GENTLE REMINDER

You belong here. The world needs you.

ALICIA JENNINGS

SELF CARE IDEA

Repeat the following affirmation: I am more than enough.

EMPOWER HER STORY

EXPRESS YOURSELF

EMPOWER HER STORY

JOURNAL PROMPT

What/who do you need to let go of? Why?

DATE

DATE

GENTLE REMINDER

Name what you need. Release what you don't need. Receive what you want. Protect your peace.

ALICIA JENNINGS

SELF CARE IDEA

Take a break from social media.

EMPOWER HER STORY

EXPRESS YOURSELF

EMPOWER HER STORY

JOURNAL PROMPT

Why are you important?

DATE

DATE

GENTLE REMINDER

Be gentle with yourself. Embrace your imperfections. Always remain authentic.

ALICIA JENNINGS

SELF CARE IDEA

Dress up and go have some fun!

EXPRESS YOURSELF

EMPOWER HER STORY

JOURNAL PROMPT

What's holding you back from living the life you desire?

DATE

DATE

GENTLE REMINDER

Give yourself permission to grow.

ALICIA JENNINGS

SELF CARE IDEA

Join a new community. Surround yourself with people who lift your mood and inspire you.

EXPRESS YOURSELF

EMPOWER HER STORY

Even when it
feels
uncomfortable,
GROW.
You're not meant
to stay the same.

EMPOWER HER STORY

Resources

I'm so proud of you for completing this journal! I hope you enjoyed all of the prompts, reminders, and activities. Here are a few more resources to support you on your personal growth journey.

BOOKS

Elaine Welteroth, *More Than Enough* (Viking; 1st Edition 2019)

Don Miguel Ruiz, *The Four Agreements: A Practical Guide to Personal Freedom* (Amber-Allen Publishing, 2011).

Sarah Jakes Roberts, *Woman Evolve* (Thomas Nelson, 2021)

Nedra Glover Tawwab, *Set Boundaries, Find Peace: A Guide to Reclaiming Yourself* (TarcherPerigee, 2021)

About the Author

Alicia Jennings is a writer and the creator of Empower Her Story, an organization dedicated to helping women overcome self-limiting beliefs and take specific action to achieve their goals. Alicia began journaling as a teen and is now teaching women how to practice self-care through journaling. She is passionate about creating safe spaces for women to feel seen, heard, and celebrated. Alicia lives in the Boston, MA area with her Fiancé and daughter.

Made in the USA
Columbia, SC
08 December 2022

72976323R00104